A Click That
Changed My Life©

A Click That Changed My Life©

Based on a true story

Victoria Vorel

To order additional copies of this book, please contact:
Palibrio LLC
1663 Liberty Drive
Suite 200
Bloomington, IN 47403
Toll Free from the U.S.A 877.407.5847
Toll Free from Mexico 01.800.288.2243
Toll Free from Spain 900.866.949
From other International locations +1.812.671.9757
Fax: 01.812.355.1576
orders@palibrio.com
299598

Contents

Dedicated to all kind-hearted people who know that love exists, that happiness is always in giving more than in receiving and that good manners will always be fashion. With love to my husband, whose philosophy in life taught me to be a better person. To the Swiss people that fought to give future generations an inheritance of values and principles that constitute one of their most valuable treasures.

Thanks to everybody who inspired me to tell this story. To Elle and Fredy who never stopped believing that this relationship would work. To my son Felipe, who always cheers me up and pushes me to go on. To my daughter, who motivated me to search for a second chance in life. To my publishing consultant, Jorge de Sauza, who gave me all the orientation and support I needed during the whole publishing process.

Prologue

Everybody dreams about finding the perfect person to share life with. Nonetheless, it is just few years ago when people started considering to go beyond their frontiers. Globalization, nowadays means, finding our soul mates on the Internet, even though it involves some risks. Anyway, if you are patient enough, you get information about everything that matters, see beyond the words and follow the deep voice that tells you what is right and what is wrong; then you can be as lucky as I am and find this lovely person who is waiting for you, who is able to complete you and bring happiness into your life.

There is an important subject you have to consider when you are determined to start a relationship through the Internet—it is the cultural aspect. It is true that there are many other things to analyze first, but if you are unable to handle a different culture other than your own, then just focus on your local web dating sites. There are numerous sites that offer the possibility of finding a partner and people can also find interesting advice on how to make their experience something positive and not suffer from big disillusions, because of not being caring enough. It is important to get as much information as you can when it comes to starting something new to people you don't know.

No precaution will suffice to be totally protected from people with bad intentions. That is why, when the moment comes to get to know each other face to face, it is advisable to hold the date at a public or open place, have some company with you, or at least people around. It is also important to schedule the date during daytime.

In case of rejection, it is very important to understand that there is nothing wrong with you, the other person just simply has a different taste and we are not it, but we could be the first choice for many others, that is why there is a huge variety of couples in the world.

My experience showed me that the fascination you feel towards other countries becomes different when you are living with a person that represents it. Let me give you an example: as I was visiting the Louvre, I found it amazing, wonderful, extraordinary, full of surprises, and definitely very interesting. It also became exhausting, until I learned to watch around through the eyes of love. That was when I calmed down and saw a different kind of beauty everywhere.

Marrying a foreigner, I have to say, is worth it because you will no longer be a citizen of your country alone, you will be a citizen of the world. Some things that never crossed your attention before, will become your constant worry. The whole planet will be of concern to you. You will open your eyes to the world.

Normally, when you go on a holiday to a certain place, you become interested in it. After you come home, you check the TV for news of the weather back there, (or anything similar to that). But being married to a citizen of that country will instill in you a much bigger sense of concern. You will start being interested on every single tidbit that is happening in your partner's place. In my case, I even got to know things about the country of my partner that not all people there value as I do.

Love is all about giving, that is what I learned since I was a little girl. Today I can certainly say that this is not just a food for thought. It is about connecting yourself with the Universe and being a part of it. It spells out the difference between being the actor and being just a simple spectator. It implies sacrifice and sometimes suffering; but what would life be without experiencing the sensations of different emotions?

It is not only the rich and famous who could have a beautiful life. The majority of people consider money, fame and beauty as the only source of happiness yet the media shows us famous, beautiful and rich people committing suicide. I have seen less fortunate people happier than those on high social spheres. I have seen some people giving out what they themselves need yet being infinitely happier than others who hoard things which they won't even use.

Happiness is a state that we cultivate more and more when we learn to give, and share. It is for this reason that I encourage the readers to search for love, charity, joy, friendship, sympathy and genuine concern towards others. Each one of us needs to be loved and accepted, as we are social beings. Being kind won't cost a single cent yet it gives back a plenty of satisfaction. If you have a partner or if you are looking for one, it is better to live each day with a smile on your face and kind words that come out of your lips. It is a gift we can give others, it is something that we don't have to buy, because kindness dwells in us, no matter how hidden or unappreciated its value is.

This is my story, it is real and I want to share it to all those who are searching for love over the Internet or to someone who is just looking for love . . . period!. I also want to share this story to all those who are just interested in getting to know my experience. This story could be interesting, just because it has a happy ending . . . at least for now.

Chapter I

The One

I am not an internet relationship guru, so this is not a manual on how to find the love of your life over the net, but this is a true story of two people that are happily married thanks to this media.

There is always prejudice towards searching for someone through the Internet (whether you're just looking for a friend or looking for someone to marry), so everytime someone asks me where I met my husband, I could spin imaginary tales of romance on the spot or anything else but the truth. This is one of the most major reasons why I have to write this book . . . to tell our story. It is not something negative, or something to be ashamed of. My husband and I are well educated and good mannered people. In fact, in my country, we are considered absolutely decent. But we were on a crossroad of our lives by which, after failed marriages and painful divorces, we decided to give ourselves another chance. We realized that there is no reason to feel embarrassed, just because we met on a more *modern* way. Maybe after a few years, this will become an absolute norm and when you tell the story of how you met, you won't cause an awkward silence around you.

Visiting a website and searching for a partner is something quite special. Nobody knows what will happen next. People, at the very least, hope not to get hurt and if they are lucky enough, they get to find their soul mates. Obviously, after your profile is registered on the net, anything could happen. Be prepared to receive all kind of emails, from all types of people with all sorts of intentions. We (I mean women) are generally romantics and sensitive beings. These qualities may not turn out to be advantageous sometimes. If our goal is a serious relationship, our future depends on how balanced we can be. In order not to fall in love with the first man who would write to us, we must be very objective. It doesn't take a rocket scientist to know that some people over the net are not totally reliable. It is amazing how much an email can do. If a person who has contacted us is a serious one, he will give us enough information to confirm truth behind what he has been saying through email. There is always a possibility of finding an angel or a possibility of finding a demon. It definitely possible to find a good human being who would deserve all our love and who would love us back; someone who would respect us as individuals.

I am Latina. I looked for a European. My reason was very simple: I was following my intuition, and I was applying what I learned from experience. I was looking for an intelligent man whom I could trust. I was looking for a respectable man that would deserve all my admiration. I believe that if we admire the man we love (specially his values), he will never cease to be the most attractive man for us.

Maybe you're thinking that I could have picked some other cultures, like the Asians or the Arabs, but those cultures are a total mystery to me, so I didn't get to pick any from both cultures. Sometimes I have thought about having to face this matter in my next life. Maybe then, I will be born as Asian to complete my knowledge and my soul evolution.

Latinos have thousands of ways to seduce a woman, but not many of them are good husbands. Sadly, they need constant reassurance of their masculinity and that is why they have the tendency to be involved with plenty of affairs. Anyway, there will be always a positive and a negative side to every equation. The positive things about Latinos is the easy mode of communication since you both speak the same language, you both have the same habits, taste in music and dances. We Latinos share the passion for dancing and when we talk about hot rhythms, no other culture can do justice to mambo, cumbia, salsa or merengue.

After a long time of meeting all kinds of people from different parts of the world: some of them very charming, some others were *definitely* not, while some were inconceivably unpleasant, I finally found my soul mate. He is an attractive, intelligent and kind-hearted Swiss gentleman who wrote me an email *without beating around the bush*, yet his email was very respectful and most of all, very honest. His letter didn't have any contents of flattery or anything that would impress me. It just had few words showing his interest in having correspondence. He let me know a lot about him. That made it very easy for me to decide to answer promptly.

We had correspondence for seven long months. At the onset, we continued being non-exclusive (meaning we still chat with other people). However, after three months, we decided to cancel our profiles on the Internet. Around this time, we continued writing to other people we have met previously. By the 6th month, we decided to stop our correspondence with others (even though they were just friends, because we were already writing romantically to each other). We took into consideration that it was not right to maintain other sorts of relationship with others who could misunderstand the concept of pure friendship we offer them.

During those days, there was a very nice man who wrote to me from the UK. He was very gentle and he wished me luck when I told him that I would stop writing because the relationship I had with some other person was turning into a serious one.

An Italian man got annoyed, while a sweet man from an Eastern European country responded that my decision made him sad, because he received my email on his birthday. It was exactly on that day that he intended to ask me to start something serious between us. His words were a big surprise to me because we never talked about love. Our communication was more informative than anything else. We wrote each other lot about our countries, customs, and traditions. We never even talked about family or anything near that.

The best lesson we got from this type of experience is being respectful towards the feelings of others. We are dealing with human beings and nobody deserves to be mistreated in any way. It was sad what happened with that man. Sometimes we feed the illusions of others without us even knowing it. I find it really sad especially that I am the type of person who never meant to hurt anyone.

Perhaps just like Kurt (my husband) and I, the majority of people that register on *match sites* already have a considerable luggage of sorrow. It is not a nice feeling to be disappointed especially at a place where we put whatever is left of our hope for happiness.

On our seventh month of correspondence, Kurt proposed to me. I felt very flattered and happy. He wanted me to move to the country where he was living at that time and that really intimidated me. While I was expressing my happiness, I also couldn't help but comment that it was never my intention to abandon my country. It was very depressing because while I know that he is the love of my life, I also didn't want to think about leaving my own comfort zone. We had a long talk over the phone and we said our heart breaking goodbyes. How could I have not thought about the possibility of needing to move to another country? I never really pondered about it. How stupid of me. It was almost obvious that something like this would happen. Well, maybe because in the first place, I never really *expected* that I would ever find love on the internet. I tried consoling myself with the thought that it is better for a woman to remain at her place.

Three days had passed and no emails. It was heartrending, but I understood why it had to end up like that. On the fourth day, an email arrived that changed my life forever. Kurt had considered moving to South America. To be able to do that, plenty of things would have to be done. We knew it would help if we were to get married so he could get a residence permit (and we wanted to get married anyway, with or without residence permits). We also had to tackle financial issues. We decided to combine our assets and plan our future together. Kurt started calling me by phone on a daily basis. We would normally talk for an hour.

It was really crazy. We had a countdown to when we would finally be together: 123, 87, 54, 23 and the day came when I had to go to the airport to take him *"home"* at last.

During those days while we were waiting, I managed to lose some kilograms and looked nice enough for a 52-year-old. *You heard it right.* I was not *as young* anymore and I also carried a lot of pain in my heart. Kurt was approaching the age of 59 and he carried with him a heavy sack of sorrow. At that point, it was a time to get excited and happiness was about to happen in few hours time. I looked at myself in the mirror and I was very glad to see how those eyes that had shed a lot of tears, were shining full of hope, love and gratitude. Waiting had ended and it was the moment to meet my true love. He was the man who trusted me and who had the vision to start a new life together, forgetting about painful pasts forever.

On my way to the airport, I thought a lot about my son's reaction. To him, it was a complete big deal to know that I was having a relationship with a foreigner on the Internet. There's plenty of prejudice and stigma as I commented before. He was disappointed when it dawned upon him that I was interested in sharing my life with someone else. His father and I separated ways a long time ago but because of social image and foundation for the kids, we continued living in the same house and interacted in a civil manner.

Before Kurt, I did not have any other love but my son and his sister. They grew up with a mother and a father that loved them dearly and they enjoyed it. I tried separating from my husband on several occasions. The reasons were typical. Wives do not have the same concept of *sharing* as their Latino husbands. My children wanted to have their father at home, so we lived for quite a long time in separate rooms. There were never any exchanges of bad words or arguing. There weren't any screaming, but there were many irregularities (to put it that way). When the kids finished their education, I asked for an annulment of our marriage. At that time, divorce had not been legally approved in my country. We made the arrangements in good terms. In the end, we were free and we lived apart from then on. Felipe, my son, went to live with his father so he wouldn't be alone. Despite the fact that my son did not like my new relationship, it was him who took me to the airport that day.

We arrived early. The airport was full of people. I waited in the crowd and I looked at the boards to check the flight schedules—everything was right. There were no delays. I started watching the people there and I could see from their faces the same anxiety I was feeling thousands of funny thoughts crossed my mind. I was thinking that maybe I could invite all those people to sing along while we wait, so that we would all calm down. Then again, I was not the right person to sing. My voice is not beautiful at all; all I had was my huge enthusiasm.

I was walking around while Felipe waited by the entrance. When the time came for the expected plane to land, I sat close to the arrival zone to see Kurt after he passes through all controls. I wanted welcomed him with all the emotion I had in my heart.

After all these months ~ he was finally there: tall, so attractive, looking around and smiling. I saw him as he went out through the big glass door, carrying a lot of stuff. He told me later that he did not see me immediately. It still makes me sad every time I recall that. I didn't want him to suffer a second more in his life. We finally met each other. It was like in a movie. He took me in his arms, swept me off my feet and gave me a long kiss. He put me back on the ground, and looked at me with those wonderful eyes full of emotion. He took me in his arms and kissed me again. No words were needed. We were just holding each other's hand while walking towards the car with his luggage. I lost count on how many times we just simply held each other in a long and tender embrace. We arrived at the parking area where I introduced him to Felipe who snapped a quick, gentle but cold *"hello"*. He doesn't normally act that way, but I didn't want to push him too much. It was somehow respectful, and that was enough to me.

Going home means driving close to an hour and a half. In the car, we just talked about shallow things. When we finally arrived home, my daughter María Fernanda welcomed him. After the introductions, we took Kurt's luggage to the room. We then gathered around in the living room to talk. Soon after, my kids said good-bye and we stayed alone. Kurt did not want to eat anything, so we just continued chatting. We looked at each other with so much tenderness that nobody could have imagined we would have problems one day, but we had (just the normal ones though). Couples always have problems, as sharing life with someone is not easy (more so with somebody from another culture). But it is worth it by a thousand folds.

We continued chatting, and unexpectedly, he took out a tiny beautiful green box from his pocket. He motioned it towards me just like the way they do it in the movies. He asked me to marry him. I could not believe what was happening. I was looking at the shiny ring and thinking to myself how lucky

I was to find such a wonderful man. I asked him to keep the ring and wait a couple of months to see if we were absolutely ready. He insisted saying that we had waited long enough. The following day, we went to the registry office to ask for an appointment—we're going to get married.

That was a magical night for me. I was there with the man I loved—the same man that treated me with so much love and care (that was something new to me). It was something I had never experienced before. We slept holding hands and woke up embracing each other. We gazed at each other for a long time, as if we wanted to be familiar of every detail of each other's face. We enjoyed our moments together in harmony and happiness. It felt like I was living a beautiful dream. Despite our many differences, we had some things in common—we love reading and we have read numerous books. Some of Kurt's favorite books were my favorite too.

The wedding requirements were simple. We just needed two witnesses over the age of 18 and a professional interpreter whose credentials were notarized. We had one day to find those people. We of course did, and we all went to the Registry Office to confirm our willingness to get married.

While waiting for the day of our wedding, we decided to visit my family in the southern part of the country. We went to say good bye to my mother. She could not believe that we were living together before getting married. That was funny considering our age. My mother is very traditional and conservative, so she took it as an insult to put the family onto that position. We laughed a lot, said our goodbyes, and promised her that we would proclaim to everyone that we would get married *very soon* to somehow justify living together.

We went to visit other relatives. We travelled by train. It was not a good idea, but since we were already inside one, we just tried to have a good time. We arrived extremely tired after a ten hour journey. My relatives received us very well. We stayed in one of my cousins' home. His wife had always been like a sister to me. His property is located on the shore of the main highway in the south of the country. It is a very beautiful property: three hectares of stunning park with native trees, a huge and magnificent house and four hectares of seemingly untouched splendor of the countryside. Kurt loved the place but the problem was the language barrier. It did not really allow him to express his himself as much as he would have loved to. Most of the time, I played the role of being their translator; and more often than not, a smile was the best way to show appreciation and satisfaction and that was enough for my relatives.

Everywhere we went, we were received with so much appreciation. Kurt got along very well with everyone despite his difficulty with the language. People were captured by his good nature and the wonderful way he delights his hosts by showing his love of our local food and customs. I have an extended family, so we travelled to another cousin's home. That cousin is also married to a wonderful woman. While there, we all enjoyed each other's company. One of my nephews took us to the coast for Kurt to have the opportunity to behold our beautiful beaches. I, as usual, cannot leave my role of being their official interpreter during the whole trip. Kurt speaks Swiss-German, High German, English, and a little French. However, his Spanish is very basic. It did not really improve significantly and the reason is simple: I speak to him in English, my kids speak to him in English too, and wherever we went, we always find people who could speak German. There are many Germans and plenty of German descendants in the southern part of the country.

One day I made a huge mistake. I told Kurt that women here worship the accent of foreigners speaking Spanish, so he should not speak it. From then on, he used that as an excuse not to learn the language.

We returned home a couple of days before our actual wedding. I had found the man of my dreams. This handsome Swiss man would be my husband in April. We would be called Mr. and Mrs. Hugentobler, and I loved it. Kurt wanted me to use his last name as it is customary in Europe. In my country, the tradition of changing names when a woman gets married is nonexistent. People here can just sign their IDs with whatever name. Their signature can just even be a line, plenty of lines, a dot, or whatever symbol they identify themselves with. As for me, I decided to change my signature on my ID card. To please my husband, my signature became *Victoria Hugentobler*.

Around this time, my daughter arrived back home to live with me. She momentarily left to give us time to be alone. María Fernanda gave my relationship with Kurt a lot of support, more so when it turned into a serious one. She arrived before we did. When we finally reached home, she warmly received Kurt. They got along very well and they constantly talked for hours about England—a country both like very much.

We got married on the 20th of April. The officer was a very nice woman and she it made a beautiful ceremony. It was especially most touching when she asked Kurt if he wanted to accept me as his wife. He answered in Spanish—a clear and emotional "Sí". That was so lovely coming from him. I will never ever forget that. After the ceremony, we went home to get a bit of rest. That evening, we had a fancy dinner on a restaurant which was recommended to us and which we had reserved with anticipation. Our family and friends loved the place. Everything was beautiful and the food was delicious. I didn't even imagine that it was the start of the greatest adventure of my life.

Autumn is a nice season to get married. It makes you want to be cozy at home when it is cloudy and it makes you want to go out when the sun shines to bless the day with a little warmth. We enjoyed the days that came after. There were so many things to share to each other and we spent hours talking about God and the rest of the world. My husband has done a lot of travelling, so I was fascinated with every story he told me about his trips. I love reading, and it always has been my passion. Reading allowed me to better understand topics which he talked about. It allowed me to somehow relate to places I have never been in and contribute to the topics which he liked to discuss.

One day he decided to cook with me. It was then that I realized that my cooking was not the best. He transformed the food into *five star* quality. It was then that I started to watch every single cooking program available on TV, but it was not until I travelled that I became a good cook. Today, I can proudly proclaim that I could cook almost everything and you can bet that it will taste delicious.

Our differences in culture made our lives a bit challenging. However, we strongly believe that it was worth it and most definitely worth fighting for. According to my husband's own words, we were meant for each other. We both had bad memories from our previous marriages and we were convinced that this time, we found our soul mate. The following day, we agreed to start the procedures for Kurt to obtain his permanent residence, which would allow him to stay in my country for as long as he wants. We already had the documents which are needed for the application. Sadly, my country is not evolved enough in respect to public service. Bureaucracy is a never ending story.

Let me just orient you a bit about the government. Through many years of the same people in power, I realized that biggest mistake they had all those time was the way they run things. There was no planning, and everything was disorganized. Nobody coordinates and the worst part of it, there wasn't any kind of control. Nobody understood what they were doing.

Huge sums of money disappeared at that time—money that the government supposedly gave to public institutions: such as public railroads, sports committee and some municipalities. The reason I have to express these comments is that Kurt would always ask me why things are not running as optimal as they should be. It was hard for me to digest and admit that most of the time, things are backwards because of neglect, corruption, and laziness. It was 2005, and the delinquents were finally captured by the very efficient police department, but the judges set them free with no charges. It was a vicious and terrifying circle.

It is difficult to move forward if we continue believing that it is normal for these things to happen. People in my country watched the news about the delinquents and they were not surprised of how things ended. That is a very bad sign. These moments force me to encourage people to travel to developed countries to see the difference.

Chapter II
The Trip

I had the opportunity to travel because a few days after our marriage, we received an invitation for a wedding. One of Kurt's nieces was set to get married in Switzerland in May. I thought that sending us the invitation was just them trying to be polite, but Kurt said that his family expected us to go, and we really ought to go. I have never been overseas before, and that complicated my life. I can just imagine people telling me how stupid I am, because Latin people in general would not even have second thoughts when you tell them they are traveling to Europe.

For Kurt, traveling was an ordinary thing. For me, it was a totally unexpected event. He announced the trip while we were on our honeymoon in my country. My husband thought that a trip to Europe would be the crowning glory of our "fairy tale" and a perfect opportunity for me to meet his family and experience his hometown. I know it sounded great, but my humble Latino spirit was scared. Our tickets were set for the 6th of May. It was impossible to tell how quickly the day arrived and how we were already at the airport boarding the plane.

It was a long trip, we had to change plane twice and finally we were in Switzerland, it was nice to me that people have to take a train from the plane to the exit of the airport. I was tired but had enough enthusiasm to look around and enjoy the beauty of that place. Kurt took my hand and guided me along the hall, after we passed all the border control and picked up our luggage until we saw his family waiting at the main door. From then on it was a carnival of feelings, hugs, kisses and tears. That was my favorite part, because as a latino woman it is very easy to me to express my feelings, we are people used to show our emotions, so when I was kissed three times by each one I felt totally welcome.

My new family seemed to be lovely people, they made me feel home inmediatelly. Within the family it was obvious that we would stay in the house where Kurt grew up. The house now belonged to Oskar, one of Kurt's brother, so it was himself who took us to the place. I could not describe in all its magnitude the beauty of all things I saw during our trip to the house, because there are no words which could describe properly what you find when you are in paradise. I am not exagerating when I say that my country is one of the most beautiful on the world, we have a mystic desert and also stunning waterfalls, but here, places and houses looked like they were a part of a fairy tale.

We arrived in Hinwil, a lovely town that belongs to the canton of Zurich and located at the bottom of a wonderful hill, the Bachtel. It caught my attention that most of the territories were not flat and Kurt told me that almost all cities in Europe are like that. Most of the streets go up and down which reminds me of the famous seven hills in Rome from my geography classes at school. I did not imagine at that time that I would come across with the very history of the continent in the coming weeks. As the family nicely decided, we stayed in the house that has been their parents' home. The three-storey house has a typical Swiss-architecture, big, spacious, and has a concrete basement which was compulsory to have at that time because of the war.

There are no gates outside the house to prevent thieves from coming in, but instead there was a beautiful garden. By the windows there were lovely pots planted with gardenias. It was amazing for me to see all those fantastic houses around the neighborhood with their beautiful gardens adorned with fairies and gnomons, it was like the gardens never end, even the houses were decorations of that magic land. The grasses all over the place were neatly trimmed, even those on the nearby small hills. Everywhere I looked seemed to be taken out from a post card. The place reminds me of a tale I usually read to my kids when they were small, because the illustrations were similar to this magic landscape, it was Nils Holgerson's Trip, written by the Swedish writer Selma Lagerlöf.

Everything was prepared for us at home. The family waited for us while we organized our luggage, after that we all of us shared a delicious dinner that Katia, Oskar's wife, had prepared. It was then when I realized that I was far from being a good cook. Time passed by very fast for me because of so many events, I had met most of my new family, I was trying to remember everybody's name and it was not be easy because nobody was called Manuel, Pedro, Juanita or María. After sharing some chats and some gifts, it was time to say goodnight and we went to sleep, it had been a very exhausting journey.

Our room was extremely comfortable, I brushed my teeth and went to bed but I noticed that the bed had no sheets. Then Kurt came out from the toilet and I asked him where I could find some sheets for the bed and he could not stop laughing.

These people do not use sheets the way I know sheets are used at home, they simply use one that covers the mattress and a beautiful duna on top, anyway I slept very well even though I was more than ten thousand kilometers far from my home and my body-clock was totally different.

When I woke up next morning I was so happy of everything I was seeing and living, I wished with all my heart that my country could be as safe as Switzerland. Europe has an advantage of 1500 years over us; this gave me the hope that next generations still have a chance to have a better quality way of life in South America.

My thoughts were interrupted by a good morning kiss, just what I needed to start a beautiful day. After a nice shower I dressed in comfortable clothes and slipped in a flat shoes, I knew that I would walk the whole day, Kurt love walking and I was sure that he would like to show me the entire town in one day. Besides he wanted to prepare our trip to Paris and Venice. He was anxious to show me his favorite places, like the restaurant he loved: La Mère Catherine. With Kurt I knew that Paradise was on Earth and was located exactly in the middle of Europe, in Switzerland.

As I expected Kurt and I walked to the town, it was a one kilometer walk and I enjoyed each centimeter of it. We went to the Post Office first and bought some post card, we wrote to my children, my mother and some friends, and then we took some pictures and went to the station. The station was full of travel magazines, people can actually take them home and plan their holiday trips, but my husband wanted to make the reservation at that very moment, so he picked a magazine and found exactly what he had in mind. He spoke with the manager in their language and paid for the trip and hotel accommodation in Venice and Paris for the next month.

In the afternoon, while we were walking around I suddenly wanted to visit a protestant church, so we went up a little bit and found a nice church; it is the same church where Cristine and Serge would be married on the weekend. The first thing that surprised me was that it was open and I commented that with Kurt. He told me that all churches, Catholic and Protestants are always open in Europe and that will be confirmed later. The difference I saw between them was their altars; in the Protestant Church the altar was less ostentatious but the churches have bigger and wonderful baptismal front full of flowers. I saw some books on the seats and took one to have a look, it was for singing and I tried my best, but my husband said that my singing would make the angels run away, so I left the book on the seat again.

I knew that the community does a lot of extra activities in the church, like concerts and other cultural events. On Christmas they are made especially for the children. Talking about children, Daniel, Kurt's son would arrive next day. I had seen many pictures of him and I already felt as if I was his second mother, he was 15 years old at that time. Kurt had told me how difficult and painful it was living far from his beloved son. We went out of the church and headed straight home, it was dinner time.

Katia surprised us everyday with her extraordinary cooking; she taught me lots of recipes and gave me some books that are my treasure—my Betty Bossi cooking books. I was so grateful of my husband's family. Katia made a big effort in making us feel welcome in her home.

The family was excited that morning, Daniel would arrive soon. Oskar and Kurt went to the airport to fetch him. Nobody has told him that his father got married for the second time, so Daniel just knew that his father was in South America sharing his life with a Latin woman. We heard the car and the whole family went out of the house to say hello to the boy. I waited in the living room, I wanted to give Kurt enough time to hug and kiss his son.

The boy looked tired, it was a long trip he just had, and his home was many kilometers away, an English speaking country. When he saw me, he gave me a nice smile, I hugged him for a long time and then I looked at him into his eyes and said how beautiful it was for me to meet him. He looked shy, he didn't speak the language of the country, he understood a lot, but always answered in English, that was great for me so I can talk to him without problems.

Chapter III

Swiss Forest

Daniel's arrival made Kurt's life shined despite the fact that he acts very strict as a father. There were many times I caught him looking at the boy with teary eyes, which also made me cry an ocean. As Daniel didn't know that we were already married, Kurt had a talk to him about it. I felt so close to the boy, he inspired me a lot with tenderness and I expressed my feelings to him when he came to me searching for love. We treated all our children the same way, with love by guiding them with discipline in order for them to achieve their goals. Actually it was Kurt who does that, I simply love them with all my heart and spoiled them as much as I can.

Usually we went out for a walk in the afternoons and I became used to it. Then we had a companion, our beloved Daniel. It was so nice to go around those country roads. Many times we met people going home and they say hello to us in a Swiss Fashion—Grüezi—Grüezi Mitenand—I loved it when they say that and when they looked at you with those clear eyes, so genuine, so honest.

At times, I would go to the forest nearby the house and I would always feel relax, no fear, nothing to be afraid of, on the contrary, a lot of peace filled my heart and I became more and more attracted to the forest, sometimes I stayed there for a very long time enjoying the beauty that surrounded me, the huge pines, the charming wild flowers, the fallen leaves, the birds, and the deers.

I have never seen a deer before; my closest encounter with a deer was when I went to see Bambi the movie. Everyday that I went there I had the same thought in my mind—This is the way a magic and peaceful garden must be—Nonetheless, it was not always like this. The amazing history of this small country started in the Swiss forests, there were a lot of battles, and it was not easy for the Swiss people to get their territorial autonomy.

I was emotional when I read how everything was initiated during the war. I could imagine the Kantons of Uri, Schwyz and Unterwalden fighting hard to be independent and the intelligent way they controlled the commerce that was transported to other regions. They were so convinced about their principles and values. It was incredible that they even defeated the Habsburgs. I was also moved by the legend of William Tell, the hero. People who founded Switzerland did not fight just for a territory like most countries did. Switzerland has only 41.284 m^2. The motivation of these people was totally different; they fought to manage their own destiny. Swiss people fought to feel proud for themselves without depending on any pressure. They wanted to give their children and the children of their children a real home, where respect and manners meant an important issue in their lives. It is better to have a little land and a clean conscience at the same time, this way doing things well is not a problem, everything is fair, just and perfect, just like a Swiss clock, precise, beautiful, perfect and overall reliable.

I feel an enormous admiration for Zwinglio, the Swiss philosopher and theologian who presented an important battle against the Catholic Church's corruption issue. Switzerland is a neutral country and it is considered as among the richest countries on earth, according to the World Bank—another interesting information to have in mind when we walk by its rural roads and meet those nice people who look at us with sincere eyes saying—Grüezi—and make us feel so welcome, welcome to Paradise.

My recent marriage had transformed my life's routine into a world full of emotions. Soon I would have the opportunity to witness a Swiss wedding and I was enthusiastic about it because of the way they celebrate it, but until then I continue with my daily walks around the place while enjoying the countryside with all its beauty, the newly trimmed grass, everything seemed to be in the right place, all the paths were full of flowers, as well as the balconies of those houses I could see from where I was walking.

One of those days I found a little mouse on the road, it didn't move. I stopped and waited and because it was still quiet I stopped beside it and caressed it. The mouse moved its little head softly and allowed me to spoil it a little more, then it ran away. I would have never done that in my life, because mice provokes me displeasure, but I didn't imagine that even mice here were so nice and sociable, like in the Cinderella tale. I thought how easy it would be to feel inspired on writing fairytales while living in this environment.

Another day I took a route that went up to a small hill. I came through the forest that was very close to our home, I liked it so much that I called it "my forest". The trees and its enormous pines seemed to be welcoming me, a squirrel came snooping around the place and it made me feel great being there. I laid-down on a mantle of dry leaves and thought how lucky I was to be able to enjoy nature this way. I looked around and saw that a tree was cut and was made into a seat. When I return back home I told Kurt about the seat I had found and he decided to go and see it. We went up to the hill and I sat there very happily, Kurt started to go around and then he put on my head a crown he made out of wild flowers and named me The Queen of the Forest. That was when my fairytale was complete.

We laughed and hugged in the middle of the forest and then we went back home holding hands. On the road we met Christine, she came to visit her parents and confirm everything about her civil wedding which is happening the next day. She said that we all have to be ready early in the morning so we could go to Rapperswil in the Kanton St. Gallen, where the ceremony would be celebrated.

Chapter IV

Christine's Wedding

It was difficult for me to sleep that night. Too many things were going on in my head. In the morning Kurt woke me up singing "Guten morgen, guten morgen . . ." and brought breakfast in bed for the both of us. The aroma of the coffee recently prepared woke me up completely and I very much appreciated the slice of bread with Ovomaltine, my favorite. The shower helped my muscles relax and soon I was recovering energies. I knew it would be a tough day, but I was assuming that I would discover new places today—this idea filled my spirit with enthusiasm.

Oskar took us to Rapperswil. The landscape could not be more beautiful so I continued living in my fairytale while we were on our way to the wedding. But I had not lived even a little part of my incredible adventure in Europe, there's more to tell. Oskar parked his Audi close to the Hotel Schwanen. I was astonished with the swans on the shore of Lake Zurich. Then, we went up along a very nice and old street and I could see the bottom of a beautiful castle. It was such a great experience to see that picture in front of me, I felt like the whole universal history came over me. I remembered my history teacher, an extraordinary woman that had the ability to captivate the entire class and transport them to the places she described with surprising facility. Maybe I have been in this place before, I thought . . . maybe, in one of her history classes.

We crossed the gate and walked on the road that leads to the castle where the couple would make their wedding vows. They had requested to celebrate their marriage in this castle with a lot of anticipation. Kurt explained to me that to get marry in his country it is necessary to go to the office of the Civil Registry and manifest the desire to do it, same as it is in my country, however in this country the officer publishes the manifestation in the local newspaper and in the Municipality board, then the couple must wait thirty-day-period for anyone who wants to present legal claims. After the given thirty days if there are no objections, the couple obtains the permission to get marry.

We came into the castle garden, a beautiful park with big trees, some of them were very old, there were lots of flourished bushes, and rose bushes were scattered around the place. We enter into a big hall which walls had surpassed centuries of paintings. I found out that the castle was created to be a fort, its construction started in 1220 and finished in 1230, the Governor of the region used to live there. He was in charge of taxes people had to pay to trade across the Zurich Lake.

We went upstairs following the people who were guided by the person that would lead the ceremony. She was a kind woman in stripes of gray and light blue suit. We can perceive the formality of the ambience, too much silence I thought, that created a sort of tension, it was like we had to do an important test and we weren't allowed to commit mistakes. It is true, it was something serious, but it was supposed to be a happy moment as well.

The room was nicely decorated, there were lots of flowers and a big rectangular table was situated at the center of the room with a chair beside and four chairs in front. Many chairs were around in front of the huge table which was where the woman invited us to sit. She sat where the lonely chair was and the couple and witnesses in front. I had the impression that it was time for the questions and answer portion, because the officer talked to them and was writing something on a huge book. After a while I saw the couple smiled for the first time, then everybody smiled, I felt a big relief, we were all happy again—it was confirmed! They are now husband and wife.

After the ceremony finished we gathered in the garden. There I met a lot of people; most of them spoke English. All of them wanted to know how we met and if I danced salsa and mambo, they were also surprised that I spoke English, how could this be possible, where I had learned it and how was my country. All those questions gave me the sensation that European people think that Latinos are rare species. I could compare their behavior with the one we experienced when a little kid made an impact to us with there abilities and it was difficult for us to accept that it was true what we are seeing or hearing. It was exactly like that when someone asked me about the economy of my country and I told that person about the level of inflation we had, the way our Central Bank took control of it, and I talked about our exports, the investment projects and the interest rates. People were looking at me with big eyes, like they were in front of an alien, so I thought the best thing I should do would be giving them a big smile and that was what I did.

I asked my husband what was in the program for the next couple of hours and he told me that we were free to do whatever we want. He also told me that he had been thinking about taking me to Zurich, I loved the idea, so we said goodbye to everyone and took a ship to the city. We had lunch while we travelled; it was fascinating to see the panorama from our lunch tables. Kurt was telling me the name and history of each town we saw from the ship.

We went out of the ship and I was attracted to everything that was on sale at the port, I wanted to buy everything, but my husband was already pulling my hand so I followed him until we arrived at the center of the city. We strolled around the beautiful streets of Zurich, the Bahnhofstrasse with its elegant stores, Cartier, Chanel, Bulgari and the prestigious Confiserie Sprüngli Paradeplatz and Confiserie Teuscher. At the last stores we bought lots of delicious Swiss chocolates that we ate while we were going to the old part of the city. We went down to the street along the river looking at the nice craft-men's shops.

We continued walking until we arrived at a store selling antique things. I thought that antiques in Europe didn't mean the same way in America, here we were not talking about hundred years ago, but five hundred or maybe a thousand, I was very excited. We went in I was fascinated with everything that was there, we enjoyed a lot but we were tired and wanted to find a nice quiet place to relax a little bit, then we searched for a church. It didn't matter if it were a protestant or a catholic church, we needed some peace. Kurt wanted to show me San Peter's church, one of the oldest churches in Zurich, he told me that it had been built in the XIII century on the same land where it was a temple in honor of Jupiter at the time of the glorious Roman Empire.

When I entered to the church, I felt almost living in the passed when it was first built. Europeans really know how to maintain what they have inherited, I was amazed watching each detail, it is difficult to describe the beauty of its interior. After we sat for a while, we abandoned the church and when I looked back I could see the huge clock on the tower, it was four past six. This is something that always surprises me a lot, every church I visited here has a big clock on its tower and they all work perfectly.

We remembered that the next day would be Christine's wedding at Hinwil's church so we had to prepare our clothes for the occasion. We returned home by train and once we were there we prepared a very nice coffee and some sandwiches, we sat in the living room and my husband told me more about his wonderful country. I searched for an atlas, so I could find the places he was talking about, I was interested in knowing more about the country, then I was searching the towns which had an important meaning to Kurt and wrote on my notebook some information about them. It was getting late so we decided to rest, this way we could enjoy the next day's party.

The wedding day was full of activity, Christine sisters arrived with their beautiful party dresses. Katia made them and the one she was wearing, this tall and slim woman surprised me more and more each day.

Hinwil's church was beautifully decorated. It was a rainy Saturday. We sat close to the corridor in order to have the opportunity to see the couple closer. Very punctual Mendelssohn's wedding march started to sound, Christine came into the church and made it shined. She looked stunning in her amazing wonderful wedding dress that was full of pearls, definitely spectacular.

I had never been in a protestant church wedding ceremony and even attended a wedding in a different language than mine, but it was not difficult to understand what the priest was saying because the execution of the ceremony was very similar to a Catholic Church wedding. It was easy to imagine the dialogues they were exchanging because of the reactions and facial expressions of the participants were having. Everything was nice and then the kiss that sealed the ceremony made the moment solemn, the promise without words was carried out by the newlyweds.

After the hugs and kisses we went to Altendorf by car, where a ship was waiting to take everybody on a nice trip around the lake and to an elegant cocktail. Being there was like living in a fantasy and I realized that I missed my country so much, it was then that I knew that we think of our roots not only when we are sad but also when we are totally happy.

Before the trip ended, someone gave everybody a colored card, Kurt received a light green one and showed it to me. On the card we found the name and address of the newly married couple across them was a space where people put their names and offer them a present. I didn't understand because I knew that the presents were already sent, but I observed how Kurt wrote something there. It caught my attention that the card has a hole on one corner and Kurt said that soon I would know the reason why. When we came back to Altendorf we went out of the boat and found a lot of balloons tied up to a rail, my husband asked me to choose one like the way the others did, then he tied the balloon to the card, at that moment I knew the reason for the perforation on the corner of the card was for.

When all people were ready someone gave the order to free the balloons and it was fantastic to see all those things flying towards the sky. Kurt was guessing what I was thinking so he explained to me that the balloons could fly far away, that way the cards could be found even in another country. The tradition say that everyone that finds a card should put it in the mail, then the couple could claim their present that was offered on it. Later I knew that they received cards from Austria and Germany, those countries follow that tradition as well. I would love that the whole world could do that.

I have always thought that traditions have something magical in them, because they not only identify a country or a group of people, but also the kind of link that reassure someone's time, a sort of strong sense of belonging which is very important in human life, as it was demonstrated in Maslow theory. Continuing a tradition is sharing the pride to be a part of something important, even the new generations can participate, that the up coming history that surrounds people with an invisible lace.

Another surprise was waiting for me, at the entrance of the place where the party would be celebrated there was a clown standing on a pair of high sticks with his legs open so people can pass under him. Inside, more clowns greeted us and then there was silence, a man came with a glass box with a snake in it, I could have died there immediately. Everybody was fascinated with the show and I cried in a corner, I couldn't believe that people enjoyed something so disgusting. As the last the show finished the man left the room and I could breathe again. It seemed that someone in the family contracted that very bad taste of a show to "cheer up" the night.

After the incident music started to fill the room, very Swiss-liked but the music was very beautiful. Kurt and I found our names written on one of the tables so we sat there. The rest of the people did the same, we tasted all the delicious dishes we were being served. Fortunately the food was very similar to the one I had in my country. I make this comment because one day Katia and the girls invited me to go shopping to Winterthur and at lunch time we passed by a restaurant that had exterior tables, there was a man having a melon and ham nicely decorated. I couldn't believe that someone could eat that combination then they told me that it is considered as a delicacy there.

After we finished our coffee, someone suggested introducing ourselves to the crowd because there were so many visitors that a lot of us didn't know each other like my case in particular. The one that started use an empty frame and put it on his face and said some words about himself, then everyone did the same, when it was my turn I took the frame, put it on my face, I smiled and introduced myself in German saying I was so happy to be there and I also told them something about my country. People smiled and clapped and I was happy, but what made me even happier was to see Kurt's beautiful smile and his eyes full of love looking at me. He was surprised like everybody and I was too. I didn't know about the presentations, my German is less than basic but I did spoke it and it was great.

When the presentations finished, all of us received brightly coloured bengal matches, these would be lighted when the couple danced the waltz. The music started and all that bengals were shining while they were dancing, it was something unforgettable, but I have to say that the magic moment was when I danced the waltz with Kurt. I have never seen a man who danced the waltz in the most elegant manner and in a very beautiful way, it was everything, the way he stood and took me firmly, the way he twirled and twirled without losing his balance. I remembered Tchaikovsky waltz the Sleeping Beauty and it sounded in my head the letter that was adapted by the movie . . . .—you are the blue prince that I dreamt of— . . . . and there I had my beautiful blue prince dancing majestically, and the music was the Blue Danube, fascinating.

Later it was confirmed that Kurt not only danced extraordinary the waltz but also his folk music. A band arrived to the party they played Swiss folk music only and it was lovely to see all the family and friends danced those joyful melodies with a lot of enthusiasm. After many hours of dancing and dancing it was time to go home. On our way to Loch, we talked about the parties we attended when we were young and Kurt told me how they danced the whole night and just drinking Rivella.

Next days we visited some other Swiss cities, all of them absolutely beautiful. We went to Lucern to visit the incredible timber bridge that has all those paintings about the history of the place. It has a very Swiss-like representation, totally clean, elegant, nice and has many attractions. I liked the sculpture of the moribund lion in honor to the Swiss soldiers who died in Paris.

One day we received an invitation from Kurt's friends to come and visit their home—an invitation that we didn't want to miss. Their house was beautiful and was as lovely as the couple who prepared a very special lunch for us. Before we sat on our respective seats in the dinning area I can't help but notice a beautifully decorated dish with rolled ham and a piece of melon along with its entire presentation. I laughed thinking about what happened in Winterthur, it was silly because Kurt joined in and he had to explain to his friends that in my culture the melon is usually eaten as a desert so he is sure that I'm going to eat the ham first then save the melon for the finale. The lunch was carried out perfectly and was shared with laughter and amazing stories in between course. As Kurt predicted I ate the ham first and finished the melon after a wonderful fondue. A couple of invitations from Kurt's other friends in Switzerland followed, of course these also came with tasteful meals that never fail to surprise me about how good Swiss women cook.

Some women in my country are very good cooks as well, however we women from my country have a secret ingredient towards our husbands. We praise them. Unlike Kurt's friends who treat their husbands as partners, Latino women from my generation treats our husbands as Kings. This is a typical Latino custom, where the husband deserves the best dish, the best place, the best piece of cake, and everything that revolves around him should be regal. This tradition is slowly evolving towards modernization, but something will never change, the way Latino women express their love for their husbands. We make sure that they'll never forget our love for them, cuddles instead of a hug and kisses instead of a single kiss. Kurt still doesn't understand why I always give him more than just a single kiss—I give him thousand kisses each day.

Chapter V
The Black Madonna

One day I walked out and the neighbors were installing a machine that cuts timber along the neighborhood street. I suddenly thought of putting my "german" to a test by making a conversation about their country. While engaged in our little conversation they have insisted that I should visit this special place that they know where I could find a "Schwarz Madonna". I told Kurt about it and he said it would be interesting for me to go and visit Einsiedeln where the virgin is.

Einsiedeln belongs to Kanton Schwyz, one of my favorite places, because of so many wonderful things that I have read about it in Switzerland history books. When in Einsiedeln, Kurt also wanted to show me a magnificent library that the monastery has. Oskar offered to take us and our Daniel as well.

We traveled early that day; the highway is in perfect condition for long trips. As we go along with the trip we were greeted with beautiful landscapes that amused me like a child. The car climbed on an ascending road and drifted into so many curves. It was a long trip but I didn't pay attention with time flying fast, the magnificent view made me forgot about time. The car suddenly was brought to a halt, it signaled that there's more in store for me that day, Oskar parked close to the church, so when I got out of the car I was again faced with another astonishing sight that left my mouth open for a few seconds. The huge cathedral stood there with its beautiful architecture—it is called the Abbey or Benedictine Monastery of Einsiedeln.

The story of the cathedral highlights a monk from a prominent family who came to this land alone. The monk settled away from people in searching of a peaceful sanctuary, he was a hermit, "ein Einsiedler" in german tongue. He brought with him a miraculous statue of the Virgin Mary and placed it on the altar of an old chapel. Because of the monk's holiness people from far away places came to visit him for prayers. The said statue soon turned black from soot of candles lighted when people prayed through the years. When the monk's visitors finished praying he was most of the time left alone. He's only companions were the two ravens that he fed; they were his immediate protectors when his life was in danger. These legendary ravens once saved his life, the reason why the shield of Einsiedeln has these two ravens curved in it.

The right side of the cathedral is filled with shops that sell a variety of religious artifacts, a typical scene with places like this. There were a lot of tourists and pilgrims that day that were as amazed as I was. If I was to narrate everything I saw there that day it would take me an entire lifetime. I will try to sum everything up by describing the most impressive sights that my eyes were lucky to have laid on. A spacious rounded sanctuary is situated at the center of the church's exterior where a golden statue of the Virgin of Immaculate Conception is positioned. If the outside of the building made a very good impression, the core of the building is capable of making me paralyze with awe. Outside is nothing if compared with the decorative materials used on the walls inside.

The Black Virgin statue in the interior of the church is very impressive. Her beautiful garment complements the expression she has on her face while she carries her baby in her arms; they were lovely to look at. The mother and child were crowned with gold that has precious stones and a cross at the top. They were adorned in a pure barroc fashion.

I slipped through a corridor that led to a narrow stairs going up. More corridors followed when I reached the top, then I took the last turn, and there it was, the library.

We entered the library which is a big rectangular room that sheltered more than fifty thousand books from previous centuries. The library's archives include Bibles from different periods. One in particular seemed to have been written by God Himself. At the center of the library there is a huge board protected by a thick glass. The board is full of handwritings documents, very old manuscripts. From the gallery a full view of a large backyard is visible.

We went down to the backyard and saw so many horses. They looked so nice and graceful when they move around. Daniel and I shared our fascination for horses, so we enjoyed being there for a while. We caressed the animals and talked about them and the way some people mistreated animals. I told Daniel about my experience that really broke my heart. I once saw a horse pulling a chariot, when the horse passed in front of me I stopped and looked the horse right into its eyes; he was in pain. This made me cry an ocean.

Fresh air made us hungry, so we decided to find a restaurant so could have lunch. We ate a Swiss specialty, "Rösti", a wonderful cuisine that should be included in my recipe book. We strolled for a while, took some pictures of the beautiful paintings one of the houses in the area had on their walls, and then we went to the car and started our way back home. Nobody wanted to talk, we all avoided to say a word about Daniel's flight on next day, none of us were prepared to say goodbye and I thought he was not either.

Nonetheless, the day came and it was painful, Kurt looked very sad, Daniel hugged him with teary eyes, I couldn't stop my tears from rolling down. The moment Daniel crossed the control barrier in the airport broke Kurt's heart completely. I knew the immense love he has for his son. I have seen Kurt watch Daniel's photo everyday since we met. I hope one day we could all be together.

Chapter VI

Three Archs

We travelled to Venice by train from Zurich. It was wonderful that we had reserved with anticipation. It was a very nice trip because the trains in Europe are wonderful. As we travelled I observed that the architecture of houses that we passed by changed as we approached Italy. We arrived in Venice in the afternoon and as soon as we stepped out of the train we noticed the Latin environment filled the air. People were smiling towards each other, speaking with their friends at the top of their lungs, and greeting everyone with ease despite the noise they created.

I wanted to check out all the stores near to the station which sells olive oil and grapa, an Italian liquor. We took the street that goes down to a shopping center towards the bridge. Across the bridge we continued to one of the main channels of the city. The Three Arch Bridge soon showed up indicating that we were close to our hotel.

The hotel was charming. We were received and welcomed by an Italian in their vernacular. The hotel decoration was in total rococo style that seemed to have transported us to the earlier centuries. Everything was beautiful and romantic. It was the start of the peek season and many tourists have already checked in. After a short rest we went out to look around. The place grew into a labyrinth as darkness crept towards the night. Even though Kurt had been there before I preferred not to roam around during the night. We can continue the next day with him as my guide.

Of course we visited Saint Marcos square and the church of the same name. However when we came there a huge part of the building was under restoration. Anyway, we were still able to appreciate its beauty despite the clicking sound of the surrounding.

We walked along the sidewalks holding hands while checking out one gallery to another, while stopping by jewelry stores and crystal shops, and while just admiring beautiful Italian stuffs around us. One of the most things that I love about Europe is their outdoor restaurants where tables and chairs are propped outside waiting to accommodate their valued dinners and clientele. These wonderful restaurants enable people to enjoy a cup of coffee or a drink while being entertained by the panorama. The crowded alley was filled with tourist from different walks of the world. Despite the diversity of the crowd, I was able to easily identify Japanese and Chinese tourists because their guides have big colorful umbrellas—so who would feel lost in a foreign country like this?

Kurt brought me in front of the Bridge of Sighs. In ancient times the bridge was used to transport outlaws from freedom to imprisonment. Once inside the penitentiary these prisoners would look out of the windows and take a glimpse of the world they once knew one last time. The sadness sighs of the prisoners that cross the bridge named the pity infrastructure.

Thinking about the sad story of the prisoners changed the expression of my face. Kurt noticed this so he took me to a mask store where masks wore these happiest smiles that will never fade. We took pictures of the masked people and this group who were dressed as allegorical characters from the carnival. The maze that this enchanting place has was not a problem for Kurt because we never seem to get lost even if the streets get narrow by shops crowding in from both sides. I really had fun shopping; we bought presents for our family and souvenir items to bring home. After the day out we headed back to our hotel. We were tired, but more in love than ever.

We took a nice shower that rejuvenated our entire body. After a few moment of rest we started to prep up for dinner. Kurt guided me down to the restaurant in a chivalry way, he's such a sweetheart. The dinner we had that night was amazing, I loved it. The hotel services were incomparable. While we were having dinner we talked about our plans for the next day. We planned to visit churches but not in a religious manner, we wanted to explore these churches to be acquainted with diverse ways and culture of the place. Normally churches reflect history very well and display beautiful and interesting artifacts that are extremely valuable. These churches are practically museums where people can visit and enjoy without having to pay for a ticket.

As planned we got up early to visit a couple of churches. It's a known fact that Venice has so many beautiful churches so we decided to visit the ones close to our hotel. Most of the churches we visited were under reconstruction. It only shows that there are authorities that maintain these huge churches and I admire them. The churches we visited displayed a rich influence of religion in the past. These were depicted on the walls of mosaics and marbles all over the interiors of the churches.

In the oldest church in the city, we were invited to attend a concert that would be carried out in the evening next day. Kurt hurriedly bought tickets when he discovered that pieces by Vivaldi and Mozart, his favorite musicians, will be played during the concert. The name of Strauss on the program also made me excited about attending the concert. The event would be at eight forty-five—I can't wait.

As we go from one church to another I discovered that churches in Venice close their doors before the rest of Europe, normally at four in the afternoon, maybe because of the reparations. It is true that Venice is a tourist destination but that's not all. It is also a marvelous heritage Italians built for their people and their future generations.

At the end of that day we were totally tired, we went to a restaurant close to Rialto Bridge, everything in there was perfect. We bought some ice creams before climbing up on the bridge where we enjoyed watching the ships from the top. We stayed there until we finish our ice creams, the best ones I have ever tasted. We returned to the hotel walking slowly and wanting to rest next day.

Of course we didn't rest, when we heard the first ship we wanted to take advantage of the time while we're still there. I was so grateful of my flat shoes; it allowed me to explore places with comfort. Kurt had bought three pair of flat shoes for me, because most of my shoes weren't flats. During the four months we spent in Europe two of my pair of shoes gave up and retired. I should give honor to them for being loyal and kind companions.

Murano and Burano islands were one of the many attractions that we could have visited, but we didn't because we didn't have enough time, so we just enjoyed their beauty in small creative objects in shops close to the center. We couldn't leave Venice without having a look at the gondoliers. We didn't take a Gondola ride because we had already spent a lot of money in Venice, so I asked Kurt not to do it, but I enjoyed watching how beautiful they look and how dedicated they are with their jobs; I really hope that people take the gondola ride because gondoliers have to prepare themselves for a long time to get their license to drive the gondolas, they even have to pass tough exams. If I have the opportunity to come back to Venice again, I will save money for the wonderful gondoliers of Venice, because they deserve people attention, I would like that the authorities could help them so they could continue their fantastic work. I have read that they don't have the possibility to live in the city. What is Venice without the gondoliers?

We ate our dinner without hurrying, anyway the concert would start in an hour time, and besides we were very close to San Giacometo Church, the concert venue. We had coffee as we talked about all the places we had already visited. Then, we walked slowly to the church. There were few people when we arrived, we entered and found privileged seats. Soon the place was full and the concert started exactly on time. I cried in silence, I was very emotional thinking about how lucky I was to be able to experience such spectacular event; I was carried away with the extraordinary execution of each musical piece. The ambience was very solemn, we enjoyed every second of the program. The participants should not leave the stage and play some more since we didn't stop applauding.

I am sure it wouldn't be wrong if I say that nobody wanted the concert to finish, because nobody left the church even after the last piece. Like some of the spectators we stayed in silence for a moment and only left when the church closed. It was a fascinating experience for me, I had gone to the opera and witnessed beautiful ballet dancers in my country, but this experience would sum everything up, obviously I was in a magical place.

Chapter VII

La Vie En Rose

Our trip continued, this time we were in the train that would take us to Paris. Saying that I was happy can't describe even a small part of what I felt that moment. Paris is just too much for me to handle. if you don't understand what I am saying then you have to ask a Latino what it means to have an opportunity to know a city which is full of romanticism—Paris.

The train stopped a few times which was building up my excitement. When we finally passed the frontier I knew that there is no stopping me from visiting Paris! After the officer checked my passport, I asked him to stamp it because I wanted my passport full of stamps. We had lunch in the train and then we slept for few hours. We arrived late that afternoon at Gare Lyon and I felt as if I was suspended on the air with so much happiness. The station was filled with people but despite the fact that I never liked crowded places, I felt fascinated walking among those people there. We went to the exit and asked for a taxi. We had reservations in a small hotel close to Montmartre, Kurt's favorite neighborhood to visit while in Paris.

Once we were in the hotel we organized our trips the next days, then we had dinner and went out to see Paris in the night. The word beautiful is too simple to describe the city. An extended vocabulary would never compensate what my eyes enjoyed that moment. You have to be there because everything I could say won't reflect even a minimal portion that I saw in that capital. Before I slept that night I thought about how lucky I was to be in Paris. I said thanks to God and then I drifted into deep sleep.

We woke up with the noise coming from the street so we got up and prepared ourselves for a tough day of walking. After breakfast we went to Sacré Coeur. We went up the stairs towards the Montmartre neighborhood.

We saw many coffee shops with some tables outside, beside the streets. There were stores all the way to the pictoresque square where the artists create their work of arts—it was located in the famous Place du Tertre. We stopped and admired the paintings for a while. Kurt then mentioned that he wanted to show me a place he loves dearly because he had wonderful memories there. It was a very old restaurant in front of the square called La Mère Catherine. We decided to visit the church first and then came back to have lunch at this restaurant.

The first thing we did when we arrived at the Basilic of Sacré Coeur was to appreciate the fabulous view we had from where we stood. The church has architecture with extraordinary beauty and is located on a small hill that dominates a huge part of the city. Many people were on the wide stairs before the entrance, some were taking pictures like the typical tourist and some were just enjoying the wonderful panorama. There was a newly married couple, foreigners, having pictures for their wedding album. With the smiles they wore that day, I could imagine how much they wanted to get married there, so I thought that the pictures they were taking that moment was a nice idea.

I was able to secure handful information regarding the construction of the church. Construction begun at the end of the nineteenth century, it was made with a special kind of stone that reacts with rain water resulting to constant production of a white substance which keeps the building's white facade, the more it rains, the whiter the church becomes.

The top of the Basilic has an Indian style going on with its design, which makes them very similar with the famous Indian grave, the Taj Mahal. Over the archs were the statues of Jeanne D'Arc and Louis IX, Le Roi Saint, personnages of significance not only for French people. The church bell there is the heaviest of all the bells in the world, nineteen tons at that, it is called Savoyarde. In the interior, what impressed me very much was the mosaic over the altar and the vitraux of the windows were the organs were. In general, everything is a beauty there.

Montmartre is fantastic because of the diversity of elements we could find there. The majestic Basilic on the top, la Place du Tertre in the middle with its constant artistic and commercial activities, and at the bottom where one of the most famous cabarets in the world, The Moulin Rouge, the meeting place of the parisien boheme.

We went to Kurt's favorite restaurant and enjoyed a beautiful lunch on one of their tables outside. French onion soup is one of the most recommended dishes there. Then we entered to have a look at the antique bar and those old walls with nice paintings and particular lamps. We stayed until late in that neighborhood. Kurt wanted me to see the city from there during the night with the lights on, and it was fantastic. The neighborhood looked splendid, then my most fascinating experience happened, it was when I turn to the right and saw the Eiffel Tower completely illuminated, it was something I will never forget.

Even though it was late, there were many of people on the streets, especially on the stairs of Sacré Coeur, mainly young people just hanging out playing their guitar while singing. We sat among them and let our hearts talked. Then slowly we went down the hill and walked back to the hotel which name is very easy to remember, "Roma Sacré Coeur", its location is also wonderful. We were received by very nice French people whose beautiful smiles were always on their faces.

The night was warm, so we weren't able to sleep very well. As soon as the sun came up, we started our adventure. We went to the metro station which was very close to the hotel. It led us to an exit next to Notre Dame. When we arrived at the park we stopped in front of the church and admired its wonderful towers.

The church has three wide passage doors for its entrance; the middle door was decorated with a rose at the top. Each door has name, the one in the center is called The Last Judgment while the other two were dedicated to the Virgin Mary and Sainte Anne, her mother. Being inside gave me a tremendous feeling of magnificence, even if it's not as ostentatious as some other churches in Paris. This church like Saint Peter in Zurich was built on the ruins of Jupiter Temple during the romans time.

After our trip to Notre Dame we visited Saint Chapelle, a small church with a gothic style. I was fascinated with its long stunning windows which were totally full of vitraux. We went out of the church and strolled along the shore under the Bridge of Sena River. After a while we sat on the sand as we watched the ships full of people waving towards us. When we were energized again we continued with our touristic journey and went to the Louvre. We bought our tickets for 8.50 Euros each and entered into the crystal pyramid, it was a horror, I meant the contrast, definitely a bad taste, at least for me.

Louvre Museum was a castle at first, then it was transformed into the King's Palace, but it was abandoned when he moved to Versalles. We visited many sections in the museum, but it was impossible to see everything in one day, so we chose to see our favorite painters, mine are the impressionists. We also admired the Spanish, Italians, and other extraordinary European painters. Of course we went to the hall where Gioconda of Da Vinci is, I was surprised that it is smaller than I thought. I would have liked to admire my two favorite paintings, but they are not in the Louvre; one is the Birth of Venus by Botticelli and the other is Montura de Caballo Chilena by Claudio Bravo, the hiperrealistic wonderful painter. I also like very much a lovely painting of Albert Anker, an extraordinary Swiss painter, Sleeping boy in the hay.

Coming again to the Museum, there were huge salons where we appreciated marvelous jewelries and crowns of France's Kings and Queens. We saw beautiful crystal objects and a vast collection of small decorated boxes.

In general we were able to grasp some ideas about the most famous sculptures because we have seen them in pictures. But to look at them face to face is something different. They told stories about a very splendorous time like the extraordinary Egyptian antiques. I loved them and I transmitted my passion for Egypt to my children. Although it didn't sound elegant, I asked Kurt to take a picture of me with the statue of Tutankamon. There was a time that the television in my country was passing a series about Napoleon's life that's why Kurt also has taken a picture of The Coronation of Napoleon.

It was late when we went out of the Museum and all we wanted was a good coffee, so we tried to find a restaurant and we enjoyed a beautiful coffee and delicious croissants. To return to the hotel we went to the bus stop looking for a route that could take us to our destination fast and we found out that the brown 95 route was perfect for us. While we were in the bus I looked out of the window and watched everything with passion, because I didn't know if I could have another chance to be there again, maybe I would never have it.

That night we slept like angels. The next morning after we organized our tour for the whole day, we went very enthusiastically to the Champs Eysées. It was amazing for me to see all those places that I had studied in school. French in my country was a very important subject in my time, we spent six years studying the language, the last three years were spent studying about the history of France and the biography of the most prominent and greatest French people of all times.

On the last year the majority of us dominated the language very well because of our teacher. I had commented this to some of my compatriots and they all coincided with me that French teachers are well prepared and have wonderful methods in teaching, they enter the first day of class speaking in French, they make their students practice the language from the very beginning, this made a huge different from our English teachers, because we studied twelve years or a minimum of six years of English but nobody went out of school speaking it.

My French teacher Madmoiselle O., besides being very elegant and beautiful, was also a charming person. Her classes were a gift for me, that is why it was such a privilege to be there, the effort she put in transmitting us the culture of the country she loved dearly should be honored. I would love to have the opportunity to meet her again. Sadly I have not heard from her since long ago.

We went to all the famous places that the Avenue of Champs Elysées has, from Concorde Square, where the Obelisk is and to the Triumph Arch. We checked out the small Palace and the Big Palace and the beautiful Alexander III Bridge with its wonderful chandeliers and golden decorations, lovely places indeed. There were a lot of stores along that avenue, as well as restaurants, cinemas, hotels, offices of some big companies, and the famous Lido.

The Eiffel Tower is something special because of its incredible architecture. I read that Gustav Eiffel originally planned to build it in Barcelona, but his proposal was rejected. The best way to visit the tower is by just roaming around Paris without knowing where it is. That is the way I visited it which was more impressive than any other ways. I didn't know we were walking towards the tower because we walked a lot that day, so I just simply tugged along with Kurt and suddenly I was some meters away from a huge metal foot, one of the bases of the great tower. We went up the stairs to the first floor and then we took the elevator, it stopped in some floors, so we had the opportunity to buy some souvenirs, then headed back to the elevator and up to the top. At the last floor there were screens where we could magnify the most important buildings in front of the tower so it was very easy to recognize each of them; there were many screens around the entire room.

There were also many flags of other countries on the top of the walls and people could see how far their country from the tower. We investigated how far our respective countries from the tower, Kurt's country was just around 400 km, mine was more than 10.000 km. Outside of the last floor there were fenced terrace with a stunning view of the city.

Chapter VIII

Schaffhausen

My secret desire was to travel to the place where Kurt was born and visit the house where he lived his first years, all those places that are so significant to him. We took another trip, this time we were again guided by Oskar. We went early so we will have the opportunity to visit many towns in the region. Kurt sat besides Oskar so I enjoyed the space and comfort of the back seat of the car, same as the nice landscape.

We were headed North, close to the German barrier, the road was full of curves, it was surrounded with beautiful fields and small villages. When we were close to our destination I was surprised by the sight of numerous vineyards through the window, I didn't imagine that people could cultivate vines with that kind of climate. We arrived at Schaffhausen and it was another meeting with history, some buildings had very nice paintings on their walls, there were extraordinary sculptures, beautiful fountains, and stunning balconies.

Without any doubt the treasure of the city was a very special monument, a circular tower, a fort, the Munot. There was a bell on top of the tower and people call it "Munotglöcklein" the same title of a song that is referring to the beautiful bell.

According to place's tradition, at nine o'clock in the evening the guard of the tower makes the bell ring that would signal the closing down of bars and city doors. Not far from Schaffhausen there is a small village that has to be visited because of its incredible well maintained houses, Stein am Rhein, to be there is like being in the Middle Ages, a beauty, another treasure of the country.

After visiting the Munot, Oskar took us around to many villages until we arrived at Gächlingen, the family cradle. First we went to the house were all of Kurt's brothers were born and a world of emotions filled the atmosphere. Everything looked so very well taken cared of; we took some pictures of the house and the fountain in front. It is so nice to see those fountains, because even though they are very old, they give each place a fresh and joyful touch with their beauty.

We walked close to the house; there was an interesting place Kurt wanted to show me. It was an empty yard behind a storage place of nicely organized cut timber. That place was their Kingdom where he and his brothers played and lived wonderful adventures. I could easily imagine a group of children running and jumping around wearing the typical garments during those days, short pants, argyle socks, and suspenders. By the way, talking about children, I wanted to see the school where they studied their first years, so we went there. Oskar and Kurt stood on the stairs at the entrance while I took their pictures. it was nice to see them reminiscing memories of their school days.

We had lunch at a beautiful restaurant in Gächlingen where we ordered spaghettis. I have never seen in my life the biggest dish full of pasta. It was more than delicious, but I couldn't eat everything completely, anyway it will be always in my mind. We have a cup of coffee then walked again on those lovely streets of Kurt's home town.

We arrived at the Church and entered in silence, I was observing everything while Kurt was talking to the priest. It was the simple decoration that invited me more. On one side of the altar there was a big rustic timber cross, just the cross, like in all protestant churches. I liked that they didn't have the body of Jesus there because it is so painful to see him suffering and because He is in Heaven and not there anymore. I took some pictures later, Kurt stood close to the cross to show how big it was. When it was the time to leave I had the sensation of saying goodbye forever, I was sad because I wanted to come again and pray for us, for all mankind who want desperately peace, so everyone could find the way to the truth, love, and happiness.

We went into the car and Oskar took us to the Rhin Waterfalls which has spectacular scenery surrounded by vegetation. The main attractions in the area were the old and big water Mill at the top of the road, the ships that take people at the center of the fall, and of course a beautiful castle.

Kurt was born in Gächlingen, Kanton of Schaffhausen and everytime when he talks about the place, his eyes shine with pride and emotion. If the Mayor of the city knew how much Kurt made the place famous, maybe my husband would receive a medal or something. In fact, every time Kurt goes to public services in my country or whenever he meet new people he tells them a lot of information about Schaffhausen, he is always talking about the place. Most of the people we are related to, could recognize the black and yellow shield of Schaffhausen. The same shield I made in carta pesta which my son nicely drew and painted with so much appreciation for his Dad Kurt.

My kids have a good relationship with their father and he love them as well, nonetheless Kurt has gained their hearts and they feel very happy to say that they have two fathers that love them a lot. On the other hand, they have two mothers that will die for them as well, because my ex husband's partner is an extraordinary woman, intelligent and has a beautiful and sensitive soul. We just need our beloved Daniel to be complete the bunch.

Chapter IX

Unexpected Gift

Communication with my kids was normally through the internet, we wrote to each other constantly; as time passed by, Felipe was changing his attitude towards Kurt, he knew how happy I feel every day having him with me and how he had transformed my life. I was grateful of the way things were developing; the whole family having so much harmony is wonderful to me.

One afternoon after writing to my kids I sat on the living room with the rest of the family that were enjoying some television program. I commented how difficult it was to describe the beauty of the country, and then Katia suggested to Kurt to invite the kids to come spend time in Switzerland. Kurt responded immediately with a lot of enthusiasm, Oskar did as well, and I couldn't believe what I was hearing. Of course I would love to have the kids there I felt so happy to know that they would be welcome to visit, I also felt overwhelmed with all that immense generosity.

Kurt calculated the time difference to call immediately. Katia passed the telephone to him and then he called María Fernanda, I could imagine her surprise. I seemed to be dreaming while listening to Kurt as he was giving directions to my daughter on how the preparations for their trip to Switzerland should be done. Maria Fernanda told Felipe about the invitation. I would have liked to see their faces right there and then. I imagined that Kurt's happy face was not just enthusiasm, but euphoria. Exchanges of E-mails were done from both ends, Felipe needed to secure a passport because that will be his first time to travel that far. María Fernanda made the reservations and when everything was confirmed they gave us the exact date of their arrival.

The day of their arrival was filled with emotions, Kurt's whole family came to fetch my kids. Emotions of joy were exerted with long moments of hug. The kids looked so happy with Kurt's family's warm welcome. There are no words to express how grateful I was to Kurt and his family. The happy faces my kids had that day will be always in my heart and will make me be forever grateful.

Felipe's Latino features caught immediately the attention of most people in the area, maybe because he had long hair at that time. I was totally surprised with his new look because he always wear his hair short. Anyway, so they were there which made me completely happy, now we had to manage the issue of communication.

After the introductions, hugs, and kisses, we four were taken to Oskar and Katia's home, where we would live the entire time we were in Switzerland. I had asked the kids to bring lots of typical products from our country as presents for the family, so the first thing they did when they arrived home was to open their suitcases and put all the stuff on the center table. Despite the fact that Kurt contributed with some money there I was absolutely grateful of the family in Switzerland to receive my kids so nicely.

My daughter never had a problem communicating in perfect English, but Felipe had never tried speaking the language, his only English were the ones he learned in school and as I had mentioned before, the English program in my country is not good. English class before only taught grammar without having a chance to ever practice them. I have also seen that many teachers gave their students papers with English writings that they had to translate in our language, and that's all it, that's basically the English class. Fortunately this is changing and the practice of the language is having a little more importance. Felipe was slowly using more and more of the English language he knew and his effort was compensated, after two month in Switzerland, he spoke quite well in English.

There were many incredible nice gestures from the family. Having the kids in Europe was one of them. Oskar bought new rollers for Felipe. Kurt's sister, Elke and her husband, were visiting their daughter and family at that time, they invited us regulary to share with them lovely moments, we felt wonderful with them. The whole family was very nice to me and my kids.

During the kids stay, Kurt asked the family to lend him two bicycles, he knew that Felipe loved sports as well as he, so he spent lots of hours riding the bike to make my son have a good time. It was more surprising when my husband went to his old school to ask permission to use the basketball court, just because Felipe is a big fan of basketball. In his last year in high school he had the chance to play in the school team and they became champions. Kurt liked to see him playing. They spent many afternoons in that school in Switzerland, my husband waited there while Felipe practiced and other times played with the students who invited him for a game. It seems that sport has its own language and no frontiers.

When Daniel was in Switzerland we went up the Bachtel, the beautiful hill. Now Kurt wanted that the kids do the same. He said that this time we would go by car, but Felipe wanted to show him how much he appreciated what Kurt had done, so he decided to go riding the bike. He knew it would be a challenge for him and as he loved challenges, he made it and it was wonderful, Kurt was so proud of him and that made Felipe totally happy.

At Katia's they normally listen to Zurich radio, we loved to listen to the radio jock who spoke Swiss-German. The radio usually plays German songs so we were surprised to hear that a Spanish song was playing one day. We listened to the Spanish singer until we were singing along with him. We knew the song so we were singing it happily. The following days the song gained popularity we noticed that the radio station was playing it constantly. So we sang and danced every time they play it on the radio. The song was La Camisa Negra by Juanes it was a very beautiful song that we will never forget. Thank you Juanes!

María Fernanda has a friend who lives in Prague which is very close from where we were. The short distance made a perfect occasion for them to meet, so both girls planned an entire weekend all for themselves. She told me that the time they spent together was fantastic. They strolled most of the time because her friend wanted my daughter to see the beauty of the city. They also spent so much time talking about their student life in England.

The kids were enthusiastic about how easy it was to visit other countries while in Switzerland. Going to other countries only take a short distance so they decided to go to Italy. They got the trip's schedule from Hinwil's station and bought their tickets so they can leave early in the morning. They came back very late but they were absolutely happy. We didn't talk too much about their trip that because it was time to go to bed, so we saved chat for next day.

Torrent of words poured out from my children's mouths about their trip the previous day. They talked most about Il Duomo, the huge Cathedral in Milan. I was so happy to see them with that enthusiasm; especially with Felipe who had less experience when it comes to travelling, at least now he was becoming an expert.

Some other days we travelled with them to France, Austria, Liechtenstein and Germany. It was a beautiful trip but extremely exhausting, there were very warm days and our long walks made us totally tired. We stayed in Basel, an intersection going to France, Switzerland and Germany. It was fun to take pictures there, you can make different countries as your background by just transferring the camera from one angle to another.

Everything we saw was wonderful! All our experiences was also fantastic, going up to the castle in Liechtenstein, the delicious apfelstrudel in Vaduz, the wonderful Sachertorte in Feldkirch, and the very nice turtle square in France. It was fascinating to see the beautiful houses in Austria and Germany, the landscape in general was a dream. It is very difficult to narrate the stunning places we visited, words are not enough.

After a couple of days we travelled again, this time to Appenzell. Kurt had taken me there before but I wanted with all my heart to show the beauty of that place to the kids. Appenzell is a typical alpine village where everywhere you look is like looking right into a postcard. We all admired the beauty of the houses with those stunning paintings on their walls. The kids were also fascinated watching the animals on the valley and they wanted to buy everything. It was difficult to choose just one souvenir to buy, no doubt that a Swiss bell should obviously be the first choice.

I would love to have a piece of furniture like the one in the video tribute to Ruedi Rymann, Dr Schacher Seppli someday. I would happily display lots of Swiss bells all over it so that when people visit our home, they would be awestruck with all their might. Talking about the song, I had never seen Kurt cried over any song, but when he listens to that particular song and the Munotglöcklein, he cries until I join in crying an ocean.

There were still many places to visit, we wanted to go to Interlaken, we like enigmas and they are precisely in that city. There is a park in the city that was designed by the famous Swiss writer and investigator Erich von Däniken. It depicted in the park his basis that supports his theory about extraterrestrial contact. We planned our trip on the 27th of July the day after Kurt's birthday.

Chapter X
Interlaken

Early that morning we took the train to Zurich, then another train to the mountain, when we were close to Interlaken, we could see the marvellous peaks of Eiger, Mönch and Jungefrau, the biggest attraction there, besides Aletsch glaciar. Interlaken is located between two lakes, that is where it got its name, the landscape was extraordinary. Europeans enjoy a lot of winter sports, so it is very common to see people in winter the same as in summer. There are many villages at the bottom of the mountain; one of them is Grindewald, a tourist destination. It is located at the foot of the 4.078m above sea level Schreckhorn and it has around thirty hotels.

We arrived at Interlaken and got on the bus that goes to the Mystery Park. We saw from the distance the big sphere in the park and already felt enthusiastic about the day we would have there. The park has seven different theme buildings and each of it was dedicated to show the secrets that the ancient infrastructures hide; such us the Pyramids in Egypt, Maya Temples in Mexico, Stone hedge in England, and Vimanas in India, etc.

Each of those building has representations that reveal the mysterious occurrence or how these structures were built. Inside they are big theatres where people can see films about various evidences that civilizations from outer space visited the Earth in the past. It was wonderful how informative the films they showed were, it kept the people fascinated until the lights were on. That is the moment when more questions came to mind, and then people can go to the other building and will find more and more information which will puzzle them, because everything is absolutely interesting and very well documented.

I was totally surprised when we entered into the Vimana building and watched the film there. It is incredible that in India people built those big structures with the same shape of a UFO.

The books Mr. Von Däniken has written were so interesting and full of amazing evidences about his theories. He has been everywhere visiting ruins and has documented evidences to support what he reveals in his books. Greek Mythology is another matter that was presented in his books and these sound very logical—the way he analyzed the subject and his conclusions.

Strange patterns of circles that appeared in a vast corn fields was another topic that was explained at Mystery Park, there were numerous picture exhibits which amazed me deeply. These patterns sudden appearance was incredible; they were so well elaborated with complex designs. The explanation of the scientists is as interesting as the ones I read at Mystery Park. It is difficult to be indifferent to all of the information there.

It was such a great experience for all of us. We paid a ticket close to 50 CHF, Felipe paid half of the price as a student's discount. We received gadgets so we could listen to the film's audio in our native language. Everything in that place was comforting so it's nice spend a day there, besides tasteful food and lots of souvenirs to buy.

It is an incredible point that even the Catholic Church has changed its view about aliens. I have seen priests with high ranking in the Catholic Church getting interviewed on television about angels using modern technology as their medium for communicating with people. If everything in the mystery park is true, that we were once visited by non-humans from the outer space that seemed to look like angels and Gods, and Greek mythology are stories about Gods that other people believed that they exist—then it is also possible that some religions in our time are based from these.

I was really surprised with everything, I couldn't choose a theme which would really interest me the most although all its scenery had a very good impact to me, especially Nazca subject that is on exhibit, I won't make comments about it, because it is so extraordinary and was well presented, it is something people have to experience for themselves. Everything was totally worth it. I know that the Park is open again after closing down in 2006. The news made my whole family very happy and if we have another opportunity to go to Switzerland again, that park is one of my favorite destinations, there's no doubt about it.

Chapter XI

A New Home

Like any other trips they would all start and would always come to an end without notifying their travelers about the nearing ends. As the famous song goes, "it is time to say goodbye". Even though I am happy to return to my beloved country, I feel nostalgic about abandoning Switzerland. The feeling I have at that moment must be the same as Adam and Eve felt when they had to leave the Paradise, they knew that they would never find a better place for the rest of their lives.

Once we came back to my country everything changed. Living in an undeveloped country is not an easy task for foreigners. I barely had noticed how bad things worked here, until I had to give thousands of explanations to my husband whenever things did not work properly. No punctuality, no security, no order, these were some of the typical barriers we experienced here. It is true that the Government made a big effort about the health system, but there were so many irregularities that the mayority of people in the country were desperately waiting for a change. It was sad for me to accept that my country is far from being developed and I cried many times because of the bad attitude my compatriots have, their bad habits, the high rate of delinquency and the lack of interest of the leftist authorities to address these problems. If just everything would have been working correctly, as Mr. Red Auerbach said—The only correct actions are those that demand no explanation and no apology-. I personally prayed to God for a big change, so I would not have to give more explanations and apologies, and I received the answer as a present for my 56th birthday in 2009.

My country is stunning and if we have the chance of having good Governance as we have now in 2010, we will advance. An Ideal Government is like the Government our current President has now. He sacrificed his life as a successful business man to be the President of the Nation. He didn't need to give all that up, he had a life of peace without any distractions, but the love he had for his country made him decide to protect us from corruption and became our leader. After a few months as our President, delinquency has decreased and employment increased. I am not in Politics, but I can see the difference very clear, when we had a woman as a President I had the hope that things would change for better, but sadly it was more of the same, delincuency was increasing dramatically under her regime.

Sincerely, before our current President, it was a shame what the television showed everyday about the robbery in the country. On the other hand the television helps people witness amazing realities, my compatriots could learn from the extraordinary way people from Taiwan managed the devastation of an earthquake that hit their country and made them suffered. After a month, they had already cleaned up the mess the tragedy left by building up their new houses with the materials they found from their ruined houses. They didn't sit and wait for help, like many people still do here; instead, they started immediately to work hard to forget that a disaster was there. That is for me an example of human dignity and that is the attitude that made them special. I have read that Taiwanese are very tough and well mannered. The characteristics that the Taiwanese have are exactly what people from my country need to practice. We are very tough and very solidary but there is little respect for the others. It seems that parents don't teach their children about these important values, so maybe it should be taught at school, so we can recover our image as educated people, the image we had fifty years ago.

In 2005 after we arrived from Europe we decided to move to the south, because of the security problem my country dealt at that time, besides the landscape there is really nice. Another reason was our desire to have my mother living with us because she was always afraid to stay in the North. We bought a small piece of land with a nice timber house and a cabin. We started packing things getting ready to move at the end of October. The house in the south needed some repair because the timbers were a little loose, someone should also be hired to do some polishing, maybe someone that specializes in maintaining houses like that. The roof for our parking area should be done before we move in.

Since my husband still did not speak a word of Spanish he just stayed home to look over the workers, I had to attend with everything we needed to buy from town, I go alone when I buy some materials, check the account, and do some shopping, and so on.

When it's possible, we tried to go to the town together so that Kurt will be able to familiarize himself with the place more. So if he needs anything he will be able to find them anytime. He did it so well that there are times that he's the one telling me where to go. We worked hard to improve our place, so we combine the time we used to install the furniture with some gardening. When the workers finished, Kurt asked me to make arrangements with an agency so he could take his stuff from the country he lived to our new home.

It is hard to explain how many things I had to do to complete all the necessary steps for having Kurt's stuffs here. I contacted lots of people, asked questions from lots of agencies, made lists and lists in Spanish of all items we wanted to bring in. I had to write letters and letters, fill a lot of forms expressing in detail what his stuffs were, when did he buy them, the year, the value, the actual condition, and after all that never ending interrogations I got the papers to start the first step. It took a month the total process and finally we received the permission to take the charge from the port here in this country. I did not know any company that could transport our things from the port to our home, so I started another researching, but this time I was very lucky. I found a wonderful and very experienced company called Tromen; they solved everything for us, for a very reasonable price and we did not have to go to any place, we just waited at home.

The day when the truck arrived was a fiesta, we waited so long to have these things here and at last everything was there in that big truck. The whole lot was perfect, it was still early in the morning and the unloading was already done. We paid the transport service and Kurt started to unpack some boxes. It was not difficult to organize each thing, because the boxes had labels in which you can see in detail what were in there, very Swiss I thought and I was right, because then I knew it was my sister in law, Elke, who did that for her brother when he announced his desire to settle in South America with me. It was very nice of her and very usual of her as well, that is the way she is, lovely and always helpful and supportive.

Most of Kurt's things were installed in the main house and my things were moved to the cabin, the reason was very simple, I wanted that he could feel at home here, so I tried to decorate the house with everything that came from abroad. Besides, each piece of furniture was a beauty, the crystal glasses and bottle collections, the paintings and all the Swiss antique pieces, he brought them all here. I was delighted watching the marvelous things he took out from the boxes and I loved to hear the story of each article. We enjoyed very much the decoration process and we felt more and more close to each other as well.

My family visited us quite often; we received help from them in many important matters. Since I didn't live in the countryside before, I needed to know or learn a lot of things, starting with the weather patterns and fetching water from a well. Of course it's the machine that makes the water flows from the pond to the house through the pipes but we were not used to that process. But soon we became experts on it, because whether you like it or not, sometimes you have to solve your problems alone.

At the beginning we used to always call a handyman to fix something until we realized that our money was running out dramatically. We realized that if we paid attention to the handyman fixing something, then we could fix the same problem that might occur by ourselves.

The time passed and Christmas came. It was the first time we spent Christmas together. My mother helped me with the decoration. On Christmas eve she sang all the German songs that her parents taught her when she was a little girl, and of course, the traditional Silent Night in German. It was a very warm day; we had the entrance door opened as Kurt was sitting outside. I was in the kitchen making the typical honey little house and some cookies while I was listening to my mother's sweet singing. I went to Kurt to give him a beer and he looked at me with wet eyes and said that those were the same songs his grandmother sang during the same day of the year. My mother was brought up in the habits of German traditions and she kept them alive all the time, my mother and my husband shared the same sentiment, for him it's like having his grandmother in our home.

Country life, when people are used with farming, it's a blessing; on the contrary, it's very hard. I have learned how to cultivate my own vegetables but suffered when the weather is adverse or the disrespectful insects invaded my plants. There is always something to do in the green house and in the garden, which keeps me entertained, the same way our four lovely dogs entertains me. We have two terriers and two German Sheppards, they are our company and joy at the same time.

My kids visit us when they have some days off. Our best entertainment is the garden when it is sunny. On rainy days, television and computer are the best distraction. Television has allowed us to enjoy sport programs, so we can see the extraordinary Swiss tennis player, Roger Federer. we also like a program called Tolerancia Cero, and lately we are following a nice series on Sundays about the wine in my country, some of them are considered among the best of the world.

Talking about wines I have to mention that Kurt love my country's wine, he finds it very nice and even though he has not had the opportunity to try the best of the best, like Almavida, Don Melchor, Clos Apalta, Viu Manet, Casa Real, Casa Marín, Montes Alpha, Don Maximiliano or Anakena Syrah, just for mention some; there is always a bottle of a good cavernet sauvignon from my beloved country on our table. If I have not mentioned some wines that are among the best it is because the list is very long, I am very sorry.

Kurt has learned to love this country and maybe love it more than any people here. I remembered that some years ago there was a rebellion of students, Kurt was so moved with the desire of young people to have a better education, so he immediately contacted one of his teachers in Switzerland, an expert in education and asked him to cooperate with the Government of my country to send successful Swiss education programs. The professor did. Kurt sent all the material to our Government and asked just for a letter of gratitude to his teacher. The professor received that letter in a beautiful envelope with the watermark seal and golden letters of my nation. It was the last recognition he received from the academe, a few months later he died.

Chapter XII

Friends Forever

Supermarkets here are open every day, so we did not have a special day for shopping—On Wednesday we went to town to buy some milk, bread and vegetables. Normally we roamed around the corridors of the supermarket to compare prices, looking at the variety of offers and finally we would buy beyond our planned budget. That day we entered into a store and while Kurt went to the liquor section I went to buy bread for the week. While I was falling in line to weight the bread I stood after an older man. When it was my turn, the counter mentioned that the man before me was a German who lived with his wife in the countryside area. When I heard the word German I hurriedly took my bread and run after him.

It was really funny the way I approached that man, telling him that my husband was a Swiss from the north of the country,

I told the man that my husband speaks Swiss German, he have no friends here and nobody to talk to in his native language, and then I asked him if it would be possible that he became friend with my beloved Kurt.

The man looked at me with big blue eyes as if digesting every word I just said, then he smiled very tenderly and accepted the invitation. I asked him to follow me so I could introduce him to Kurt. When they were faced to face, I announced to Kurt that this nice man is now a friend. They started talking and talking, so I continued with my shopping alone until I was totally ready to go home. I came back and found the two men still talking so I got myself noticed with a smile while waving my hands full of bags, they both understood that it was time to leave.

We said goodbye and thanks to our new friend, we got in our car at same time and left. Kurt asked me why never told him that I had a nice German friend here, and then I realized he didn't imagine that I followed a stranger and asked to become his friend. After I explained to him how things really happened he laughed and laughed and looked at me with teary eyes out of laughter. We both laughed and I just said, "I do love you very much".

On Thursday our new friend Günther called, I passed the mobile phone to Kurt, and they talked for a long while. When Kurt got off the phone with Günther, he told me that we were invited to spend a day at Günther's house next Saturday—in two days time. His wife wanted to meet us and he added that she was from this country, so the meeting would be very interesting because we were two couples about the same ages and composed by a local and a foreigner. We were excited thinking about that nice invitation and how soon they planned it. I told Kurt about our traditions here before and now he's experiencing one of them after receiving the invitation.

Early Saturday we bought a beautiful wine, chocolates, and flowers. We came on time at our friends' house. The directions they gave us on how to get there were so clear and it was very easy to find the house. The gate was opened, Kurt drove through a nice road surrounded with beautiful pines, and soon we were in front of the house. When we went out of the car, our friends were there waiting for us. Günther's wife welcomed us very nicely. We said hello on a very affectionate way and we entered into their house. We felt a very welcoming warmth around that wonderful and cozy home.

Once inside the house the very beautiful Iris already invited us to the table which was nicely decorated. We washed our hands and sat at the table. Everything was delicious.

Iris is a teacher, whenever she comes home from school she would immediately work in her garden. All the salads we had for lunch were harvested from her garden. The wine they served was well selected and the desert was organic fruit from their own trees. After lunch Iris prepared a delicious grain coffee and we continued talking and talking. I helped her with the dishes and when everything was clean we joined our husbands who were enjoying an interesting conversation in German.

Iris and I talked a lot about gardening and cooking, we walked a little around the house. Around five o'clock, she set the table again, this time for a cup of tea. In my country we call tea time "once", which means the number eleven, we have *once* around five or six everyday. The term *once* came from the miners in the north of the country—a desert place. The temperature in the afternoon decreases a lot so miners would have a drink around five or six to cope up with the cold atmosphere. Their drink is made of distilled fermented grapes skins from the residue of wine processing which is called aguardiente. So as not to gain a bad impression whenever they wanted to have a drink, they preferred to say that they were going to have *once*, because *aguardiente* has eleven (*once*) letters.

Us and our new found friends visited each others' houses regularly, our friendship grew stronger. We enjoy each others company very much that is why we suffered a lot when Günther felt ill and had to be operated. But we jumped happily when he came home from his operation. He was pale but he still has his nice sense of humor. During these past few years we have known that Iris was disappointed with the way the selection of school directors went. She failed to get the position she applied for a couple of times because even though she was the best qualified she didn't have political alliances, (she is not in Politics). Now that the country has a different and better Government, it is too late because it was time for her to retire.

My friend received her degree when she was very young and started teaching in rural schools for the poor people in the countryside. She came in as the School Director of a very small school and years later she gave the community a bigger school with a place where children can stay and live at school in case of their homes were too far away. It was the pride the people there.

Wherever she teaches she would leave her mark. Every year she's in charge of a class that will take a special exam, this exam is also taken by other students from different schools all over the country, and the school that will have the highest average will be recognized. One year her class had the best marks. My dear friend Iris was confronted with injustice, she breaks down whenever she sees that parents are not supportive with their children's education or the bad habits and manners children have nowadays, but what bothers her more is the neglecting attitude some teachers have. There are still a lot of things to do for this country; I would like to meet other people like Günther and Iris, so honest and generous, with high values, people that would work hard to have a future, extraordinary people, beautiful souls.

The best thing about my country is that people here are joyful, affectionate, and united. Our geography is divine! We have wonderful sky lines and beautiful beaches, our wines are among the best of the world, Universities here provide excellent professionals that are extraordinary well qualified abroad, the social system is very good, the economy is now stable and growing constantly, and we export almost all kind of products, minerals, fruits, wines, fishes, grains, etc.

The bad side of the country includes environmental abuse, outdated justice system, increasing street crime incidents involving teenagers, shallow television shows which is very sad because some personalities are very intelligent people, public services have so many inefficient people, it seems that these people were chosen out of political connections.

Before the previous President left, she signed a document which assured 400 of her people in public positions, it is a shame, because if they were good workers, they didn't need to be tied to the chair.

Thanks God now the new President elected his collaborators among the best professionals on each matter, not all among the politicians like it was the custom before., we had in the past the same politicians as Ministers who rotate from one Government to the other of the same line, during 19 years, it is imposible not to think that there were much more qualified professionals to be in their position. Politics is a greedy thing!

Chapter XIII

The Magic About Respect

Probably some people won't like this chapter, unless if they read until the end. This chapter may even change their lives forever and have successful relationships. The mayority of us think that we are perfect when we interact with other people; we show off that we are educated, nice, and gentle. But are we?

Those qualities are excellent no doubt, but are we also tolerant, compassionate, generous, and respectful? Well, if we are respectful, then we should also posses the other good qualities.

The conflicts between couples and international conflicts share the same problem, the lack of respect. If we only take a little time to analyze little problems in life then we will realize that most of them happened because respect was neglected. If I would tell you that your life will be much happier and you have the power to make other people happy by just practicing the magic of respect, maybe you won't believe me.

Respect is the most valuable lesson I learned from life and lives that surrounded me. We Latinos have suffered and have been mistreated many times through history and that have made us confuse respect with submission and fear.

The old generations had a saying that is difficult for me to translate into English, it was something like "children only learn if blood is involved", of course there is no need for blood that is why we were educated in an environment full of "respect". Not more than thirty years ago, the punishments that were done to many children at school were so severe that they suffered physically. Parents accepted these practice because they believed that teachers were educated properly to know what they were doing—this seems crazy, but these things happened.

When my daughter was five years old I sent her to a catholic school ran by nuns, it was a very prestigious institution. She was there for not more than a month. She had learned a lot before going to school, so she became bored in classes that a nun hit her head every time she was distracted, she told me that one day so I came to ask the Superior for an explanation, then she gave me an incredible answer, the nun said that nobody would hit my daughter if she was only focusing during discussions. Obviously I took my daughter with me and transferred her to another school.

However the other school was not better than the last because even though they don't hit children they never support their efforts. My daughter always got the first honor in school every year until she finished the High School. When she graduated we, the parents, were the ones who decided to give her a present for her magnificent work. The school didn't do anything, not a word.

Nowadays things have changed about punishments in schools. I have seen on television that teachers are now afraid of students. This happened because most people of our generation didn't teach our children to respect the teachers and as a respond to the abusive teachers in the past. Today people believed that if they resort to rebellions they have the power to do things so most people rebel. That has happened thousand of times through history and nobody learned anything. That is why our history is cyclical. Fortunately there are still people that use their brains and find better ways to confront everyday challenges.

According to the Spanish dictionary to respect and respect have two different meanings. It may sound weird but the dictionary says that "to respect" is to admire, to love, and to show reverence while "respect" is obedience, submission, and to surrender. Anyway it is not my intention to criticize but I just want to share something I learned from a very intelligent, beautiful, and wise person, my daughter, María Fernanda. The following three questions below were the things she sometimes asked me whenever I mentioned to her the conflicts I have experienced.

1.) Are you tolerant enough with the limitations that others have?

We have talked that not all people have the same abilities. This is true especially when we were in our music or gymnastic class. Is it fair for students who do not have beautiful voices or have athletic bodies to get low grades?

2.) Do you consider both sides of the medal or are you acting on prejudice?

Normally people react according to their upbringing and don't accept other views, if we consider that there are many facts that could make people act or react on a special way then we could understand their perspectives better.

3.) Are you honest to others without hurting or humiliating them?

We can be very sincere, there are lots of kind words that dictionaries offer us to say what we think in a respectful way without harming anybody. Every time we are in trouble, we can reflect from those questions so we will know the best way to respond to others and understand them better.

Chapter XIV

Prophecies

The whole world was shocked about the incredible events that happened a few years ago, never ending wars and terrorist attacks, earthquakes, typhoon, and tsunamis destroyed cities almost everyday. Who is behind all those events? Obviously it is the man who provokes everything directly like the first cases or indirectly like the second ones. People are afraid and want to know about the future, more than ever. These series of terrorist attacks happened because few people want to take control of other countries as if they were better than the ones who were already leading these countries—this made people lost confidence on their own Government. My husband and I have read a lot about this matter and also would love to know what will happen in the near future.

Today people have the opportunity to have access on all information they want through the internet, even the most controversial and sensitive topics, they didn't care if these informations are real or fake, called Andinian Plan, Illuminatis, Reptilians, Pandemic Vaccine Business, HAARP Project, Vatican Rich Investments, all these topics are just on a click of a finger nowadays.

Most of the people have also read about Maya Prophecies and what they revealed. It is also not unknown how scientists have warned the population about Global Warming and Ecosystem Destruction. So, we, common human beings feel confused, unsecured, frustated and worried. These are too much emotions, then most of people simply take them out of their lives and decided not to think about them and follow their lives without doing anything positive, but complaining every time something affect them directly.

My intention at this point is make people think about what they hear. There is a saying in my country: "When the river makes noise is because it is carrying stones", it means that something is happening. We need to be prepared for next weather changes we have provoked because we neglected and abused of the planet. We have to be prepared for next catastrophes those changes will provoke. We have to be prepared to assume the cost of the big mistakes we have allowed our Governors to commit, but the most important thing is that we have to be prepared to assume our own mistakes.

After reading thousands of prophecies and predictions, from all kind of sources, mystics, religious, scientifics, etc., we trully believe that nothing wrong will happen to the people who act from the heart. If the people we love leave this world is just because they finished their mission here. We have to cry if they didn't do it well, we can cry if they were not able to love the others. This is a book about love, a beautiful and real love story and it is not a lie that it will be love what will save the world, so I strongly recommend to focus on it or at least give it a space in your life.

When we have the ability to understand that all our actions have consequences and most of the things we experience happen because we deserve them or we need to have them to evolve, then we will stop seeing the little errors of the others and we will start seeing the big ones we make. I strongly believe that bad experiences should make us better people and if we continue being bitter, jealous, and envious with others and continue to have a bad heart, then we have not learned anything. I lament that I don't have the capacity to explain why things happen, but I can say that everything has a reason, but it is beyond my understanding, nonetheless I have no doubts about the perfect way Universe and its system should be working.

If we have the ability to be positive, trying to keep high spirit, smile more and complain less; understand that there are no enemies, just human beings, better or worse, human beings, then we won't be afraid of the future. People will harvest what they planted. If adversity knock our door and we think that we were doing everything well, then it is time to analyze, maybe we neglected something, probably without a bad intention and the knocking on the door is just to give us a chance to correct it, to be even better.

I love prophecies, because they alert us, they make us rethink our points of view and beliefs, they warn you to take some time to check your priorities. If they wouldn't exist we would continue our lives without questioning anything. It is good to stop sometimes and even though we won't be able to change the past, we can improve the future.

Look at the past and then you will know certainly how your future will be, what we have made in the past will pass the bill in our future, be prepared and don't make the same mistakes again and again.

The best way to face what is coming is not building a bunker and hide in it. The best way is trying to discover the things that we have done wrongly, to compensate them now. If we have hurt someone in every way we didn't realized, it is still the time to say sorry, to repair the damage and it is still the time to forgive as well. We have a big chance to balance our lives, don't lose this opportunity, because maybe harmony, happiness and peace are just a word far from us, please say that word.

Epilogue

Love is something wonderful, no doubts—the difficult part is finding it. I am convinced that if we get up every morning with a smile on the face and show it to all the people we find on our way, we will have more possibilities to find love.

The reason is very simple, when we are gentle with others, normally they will be nice to us as well, and if the moment comes that they have to choose a stranger to invite into their lives, they will choose us. It doesn't matter if he or she is the one selling us a Bingo Cards or the ones who invite us to a party. Kindness generates positive feelings and confidence the same as mistreating generates anger and bad feelings. The question is which side we would want to be?

I considered a very interesting and wise advice Kurt received from his father. He said to him that before acting he had to think about the consequences his actions would give in return and if he still feels peace in himself, then he would follow his decision, so the next day he could look at the mirror and smile. Kurt and I have acted sometimes without thinking too much and the consequences have been sad, but each day we practice more that intelligent recommendation will bear the good consequences of our actions and it is true that we smile more.

This is my wonderful love story! The trips I had to those beautiful Swiss cities, the countryside I went, the Swiss forest that was full of magic, have showed me that Eden Garden exists and that it is never late to be happy. I am a Latina and this is what I am, an emotional Latin woman, I don't want to pretend to be different from who I am. Each day I become a better person because of Kurt, my beloved husband, my internet lover.

www.ingramcontent.com/pod-product-compliance
Lightning Source LLC
Chambersburg PA
CBHW051209050326
40689CB00008B/1245